YOUR KNOWLEDGE HAS VALUE

- We will publish your bachelor's and
  master's thesis, essays and papers

- Your own eBook and book -
  sold worldwide in all relevant shops

- Earn money with each sale

Upload your text at www.GRIN.com
and publish for free

Sulagna Mukhopadhyay

Learning to read. On Indian Literacy

GRIN Verlag

Bibliografische Information der Deutschen Nationalbibliothek:

Die Deutsche Bibliothek verzeichnet diese Publikation in der Deutschen National-
bibliografie; detaillierte bibliografische Daten sind im Internet über http://dnb.d-
nb.de/ abrufbar.

Dieses Werk sowie alle darin enthaltenen einzelnen Beiträge und Abbildungen
sind urheberrechtlich geschützt. Jede Verwertung, die nicht ausdrücklich vom
Urheberrechtsschutz zugelassen ist, bedarf der vorherigen Zustimmung des Verla-
ges. Das gilt insbesondere für Vervielfältigungen, Bearbeitungen, Übersetzungen,
Mikroverfilmungen, Auswertungen durch Datenbanken und für die Einspeicherung
und Verarbeitung in elektronische Systeme. Alle Rechte, auch die des auszugsweisen
Nachdrucks, der fotomechanischen Wiedergabe (einschließlich Mikrokopie) sowie
der Auswertung durch Datenbanken oder ähnliche Einrichtungen, vorbehalten.

Imprint:

Copyright © 2011 GRIN Verlag GmbH
Druck und Bindung: Books on Demand GmbH, Norderstedt Germany
ISBN: 978-3-656-52548-6

This book at GRIN:

http://www.grin.com/en/e-book/262294/learning-to-read-on-indian-literacy

GRIN - Your knowledge has value

Der GRIN Verlag publiziert seit 1998 wissenschaftliche Arbeiten von Studenten, Hochschullehrern und anderen Akademikern als eBook und gedrucktes Buch. Die Verlagswebsite www.grin.com ist die ideale Plattform zur Veröffentlichung von Hausarbeiten, Abschlussarbeiten, wissenschaftlichen Aufsätzen, Dissertationen und Fachbüchern.

Visit us on the internet:

http://www.grin.com/

http://www.facebook.com/grincom

http://www.twitter.com/grin_com

Introduction:

"Acquiring literacy is an empowering process, enabling millions to enjoy access to knowledge and information which broadens horizons, increases opportunities and creates alternatives for building a better life" (**Kofi Annan**)

This message restates that basic education is the bedrock to do away with poverty and all other social miseries existing in the modern world. India, a multi-lingual, multi-cultural and multi-religious country, is divided into 28 states and 7 union territories with a population of 1.15 billion (according to Census Report, 2010). Though a developing country, the country's economic power is growing steadily providing jobs for the citizens and India claims an international acknowledgement as 'knowledge superpower'. But poignant as it could be, India has the largest illiterate population in the world. Professor Amartya Sen has delved into this issue last year at a conference held in New Delhi. He commented, "...it is clear how much needs to be done and can be done to change the organizational structure of school education and basic health care. "[1] He has cited the example of Japan. According to Sen, the Fundamental Code of Education in that country was issued in 1872 and by 1910, the nation was almost fully literate. By 1913, they were publishing more books than Britain and twice as much as the United States.

Various causes added to the poor growth in literacy rate in India. There is a clear distinction between the literacy of the urban and the rural areas. It was found out that in spite of the progress of the quantitative expansion of education in India, multi-level inequities within the education system is remarkably sharp, leading to low growth in rate of literacy. Inequities are more complex among women belonging to Schedule Castes and Schedule Tribes and Other Backward Castes in the rural areas of the backward regions. The Indian Social Institute has identified in a research on schooling three major obstacles. They are: (a) lack of proper parental motivation, (b) poverty and (c) poor schooling standard. With the aim to overcome these hurdles, the 86th Constitutional amendment under Article 21A passed in 2002 has made education a fundamental right for all.

The Indian definition of 'literacy':

In a 'developing' country like India the term 'literacy' is measured by the rate of literacy, which is the percent of the population, mainly the adult population. The NSSO (National Sample Survey Organization) conducts surveys once in every five years to collect data on literacy rate and other socio-economic issues. The NLM (National Literacy Mission) designs, executes and monitors programs on literacy and prepares guidelines for literacy assessment. The NFHS (National Family

1

Health Survey) provides database on literacy and other socio-economic factors based on sample study of the households.

The definition and the method of assessing 'literacy' by the Census of India, NLM, NSSO and NFHS differ widely. The 'literacy' as defined in the Indian Census is the ability to read and write with the understanding of a language. The National Literacy Mission, which was set up on May 5, 1988 by the government of Indian with the mission to eradicate illiteracy in the country through teaching functional literacy to non-literates, has gone beyond this rudimentary definition of 'literacy'. Its aim was not just to make every citizen of India self-reliant in the 3R's (reading, writing and arithmetic), but also 'the ability to apply them to one's day-to-day life.'

The growth rate in Indian literacy:

We all know that the problem of literacy is faced by both developed and developing countries. Illiteracy is a problem faced by developing countries mainly due to socio-economic conditions. The post-independence Indian government took the pledge to reach 100% literacy within forty years of Independence. But its dream remained far-fetched. Article 45 of the Indian Constitution says: **The State shall endeavor to provide, within a period of ten years from the commencement of the Constitution, for free and compulsory education for all children until they complete the age of fourteen years.** But the 2001 Census report projects that Kerala has the highest rate of literacy with 90.9% and Bihar has the lowest, i.e. 47.5%. West Bengal, the highest populated state in India (8, 01, 76,197 million as per 2001 census report), and once considered the 'elite' state of the nation has only68.64 % literates.

There are even dramatic differences between male and female literacy rates by place of residence. The GPI (Gender Parity Index) shows the gender gap in literacy. There is also gap between women from urban and rural areas. In 1991 the literacy rate among urban females was twice the rural ones. Kerala has now the highest rate of women literates followed by Mizoram. On the other hand, states like Bihar, Uttar Pradesh, Rajasthan, West Bengal have less than 30% women literates. U.P and Bihar together have almost 63 million illiterate women. The gender gap in literacy rate of Indian population in the age group of 15^+ still continues to be high. Even after 64 years of Independence poor families prefer keeping their girl child at home to take care of younger ones or to help their mother in the household chores.

There are more than 400 Schedule Tribes (STs) in India. According to the Census Report of 2001, while the STs constitute 8.2% of the total Indian population, the Schedule Castes (SCs) comprise of 17.16%. Article 46 states: **The State shall promote with special care the educational and economic interests of the weaker sections of the people, and, in particular, of the Scheduled Castes and the Scheduled Tribes, and shall protect them from social injustice and all forms of**

exploitation. Unfortunately, both the Schedule Castes and the Schedule Tribes still face discrimination from the upper castes in many Indian states and they remain away from the main stream of the Hindu society. Dreze pointed out "educational disparities, which contribute a great deal to the persistence of massive inequalities in Indian society, also largely derive from more fundamental inequalities such as those of class, caste and gender," (Dreze, 2003: 982). There is dominant need for making rapid progress in living standards, health, education and other socio-economic factors of Schedule Castes (SC), Schedule Tribes (ST).

Articles 29 and 30 of the Indian Constitution guarantee the minorities of secular India like the Muslims, Sikhs, Parsis and Buddhists the right to conserve their language, scripts, culture and also allow them to establish and administer educational institutions based on either their religion or language. The key factor responsible for the backwardness of the minorities in India, especially the Muslims, is the lack of access to the common school system. Syed Najiullah says, "… the literacy rate among Muslims is lower that all the religious communities in India. The literacy rate for women is further low. It is also less compared to the all India literacy rate…..".[3] For the welfare of the minority groups the Indian government has framed a five-point program, which takes care of the appropriate representations of the minorities in governmental organizations and also pays attention to their economic and social development.

The Right to Education Act, 2009:

In 2008, the EFA (Education for All) Global Monitoring Report published by UNESCO suggested that by 2015 each child in this world should be literate. India had to react to this agenda of UNESCO. In 2009 the UPA government passed the RTE Act. According to Right of Children to Free and Compulsory Education Act, it is obligatory for each child to attend a school in the neighborhood. As per the government, out of 22 crore children in the applicable age group, 4.6%, (around 92 lakh), are school drop-outs for various reasons. The UPA Education minister Mr. Kapil Sibal has ordered the school management committee or the local authority in different states of India to look into the matter. Some of the main clauses of this bill are:

- The State shall ensure a school in the neighborhood of each child. The school must maintain certain minimum standards as defined in the bill.

- For children living in small hamlets with no school facility in the neighborhood the State government or local authority shall make adequate arrangements like transport, residential facilities and other such facilities for providing elementary education in a school.

- Government-run schools must provide free education to all these children and the private-run schools shall reserve 25% of their seats for them. No capitation fee or entrance test in private schools for these children will be permitted.

- School Management Committees or local authority shall identify children who require special training and organize them for the benefit of such children. A child with disabilities shall be provided free special learning and support material.

- The School Management Committee shall be constituted in every school, 75% of which will be from among parents or guardians of children, 1/3 members from among the elected members of the local authority, 1/3 from among teachers from the respective schools and the rest 1/3 from among the local educationists or children in the school, subject to the decision of the parents in the committee.

While the Bill focuses on the needs of women and older children (especially girls), who have to quit work and schools respectively to take care of toddlers at home, it ignores the age group 0-6 years known as ECCE (Early Childhood Care and Education). There is no Montessori or Kindergarten schools run by the government, where the children from the poor families can go. All the government schools function from Class I. the private ones are admitting children of 3 years old. The government is now proactively giving importance to the ST in addition to SCs and OBCs for the overall development of these communities.

West Bengal:

Among the different states in India, West Bengal is one such state which has taken a back-seat in the literacy drive. Calcutta, the capital of West Bengal, was the first capital of The East India Company and in the nineteenth Century, this city was respected as the abode of Indian intellectuals.

Situated in the eastern part of India, West Bengal is the fourth most populous state of the country and also the seventh most populous sub-national entity in the world map. Kolkata is the second largest city of India and it is the primary economical hub of both eastern part of India and also the north-eastern states. The minor communities include besides Muslims, Chinese, Anglo-Indians, Tamils, Telugus, Nepalese, Gujaratis Armenians, Jews, Tibetans, Punjabis and Maharashtrians. No other state in India has such diversified demography. The primary language of this state is Bengali, but English and Hindi are also widely spoken and learnt by the dwellers of this state. A majority of the Schedule tribes live and work in the different districts of West Bengal. The major problem in the rapid growth in population in this state is the Muslim refugees from Bangladesh, entering everyday crossing the border

4

in search of food and shelter. In West Bengal, where the total rate of literacy is 68.64 %(Census Report, 2001), the Muslims constitute about 57.47%, far below the average literacy rate and the Muslim girls are falling much behind their male counterparts.

Governed since 1977 by the Communists, West Bengal is an interesting state for research as it is a state, where in schools children have the scope to learn Hindi as mother tongue besides Bengali. The main inhabitants are Bengali. It is also the home for Gurkhas, Nepalese, and tribes like Santals, Kol, Koch-Rajbanshi and Toto tribe.

The schools in West Bengal are divided here into government-run institutions, private-run ones and also by minority religious groups. Under the private-run organizations, we have schools owned by Indians, the medium of instruction being English, also schools run by people who once came here on business purpose like those from southern part of India or from the state Gujarat and even Punjab. Besides, there are a few International schools falling under this category. The religious schools like Khalsa (run by the Sikhs) has an autonomous body but the Madrasah schools are mainly under the aegis of the state. The Madrasah and the Khalsa schools are run by respective seminaries and the religious scripts form a part of the curriculum alongside their languages Urdu and Gurumukhi.

As an inhabitant of this state and the city, I did a survey of the schools on how they are taking initiative to make the children of today the citizens of tomorrow. I met principals, head mistress, managing committees of schools and NGOs and parents of some children. An analysis of their views will give us an idea of our project *How Does the World Read*. Here is an introduction of those institutions and the educationists:

- Chetla Girls' High School, a state-run Vernacular based urban institution in the southern part of Kolkata since 1937 with 1184 girl-students,

- Ahead, a private- supported rehabilitation and research institute for mentally challenged children, working in this field since 1979 and situated on the southern fringe of the city. They have children both from upper and middle class society and a few from lower middle-class,

- Wahed Memorial G.S.F.P. School, a high-school established in 1944 with 500 odd children, from the slum area around the school,

- The Force for Rural Empowerment and Economic Development (FREED) is an NGO with a wide range of projects on girl-child of tribes and other backward classes living in the districts of Bankura, Purulia, West Midnapore and North Bengal, staring from education till making them economically independent and self-reliant, and

■ South Point School, the first private-run English-medium co-educational school since 1954 in the state of West Bengal catering to 12000 students. It caters to children both from the upper and middle strata of the society.

Chetla Girls' High School: Mrs. Satyabati Nadkar(Head Mistress of the senior section of the school)

○ What does the typical school day look like?

My school starts at 11.00. Before that there is a general assembly. The girls assemble at the Assembly Hall at 10.45 and they sing a prayer song. After that they go to their respective classrooms and the classes begin at 11.00.

○ After certain time, they have their tiffin-break.*

Yes, after four periods of 45 minutes duration each, they have their recess.

○ Since it is a government school, do the children get here any mid-day meal everyday?**

Yes, there is a provision fro mid-day meal. The rice is provided by the government and they give us Rs.4.00 for each student.

○ How many students are there?

There are more than 1100 students. The actual figure is around 1184.
○ So each child gets…..

No, not , not all the students. The government provides mid-day meal for only classes V-VIII.

○ And the rest?

And the rest, they don't get their mid-day meals from the school.

○ What are the learning materials provided to young/ adolescent learners?

Actually, the government provides us with a book-grant. They get some text books from the school. There is no other provision provided to the students by the government or by the school. We do not get any grant for that. There are certain TLM (Teaching-learning grant) provided periodically by the government after two/three years. We get a sum of Rs.5000.00 only from the government. But we run a parallel school fund, and the fund is raised from the students. With these the students are provided school uniform, shoes, etc. from that. And certain medical allowances are also given from that.

○ What kinds of technology, if any, are students using in their early years?***

Actually there is no technology as such which they are using in the classroom. But there are separate units like the computer lab, they classes there. They practice computer there. But for general learning, there is no technology that is used.

○ Do you at all have students with special need in your school?****
Actually, I have three students. One of them is visually impaired, the other one is handicapped, she cannot walk properly, and the other one neither can hear nor speak. She has been provided with a hearing aid. Now that she is hearing, she is developing the art of speaking also. But gradually.

○ How do you accommodate these children?
Actually there is no scope for making special accommodation for these students. So, inside the classroom the teacher takes special care to make them learn the subjects.

○ But what about this child who is visually impaired?
There is no special mean. She can read from the book, but she requires spectacles for that. They actually get a grant from the government and the school has to vouch for them that they have certain disabilities. Now we have also made government issue cards for them. They have different cards, which they can show at some hospitals, so that they can get some aids.

○ How are differences in language and dialect addressed in school?

The children speak Bengali in our school and the medium of instruction is also Bengali. The students stay in Kolkata. So they use the same language and dialect like the teacher, and which is also similar to the books also, and all the medium of instruction. So there is no trouble in that.

o What are the major beliefs regarding language and literacy? Which drives are practiced in the classroom? *****

There is actually no such special norm regarding literacy that we follow in the classrooms. But most of the students of our school are first-generation learners. Their fathers or mothers do not write or read. We have to take special initiative, so that they take the learning-process seriously. Otherwise in order to realize the importance of studies in their lives, the teachers make them aware of that in the classrooms, and there are certain periods allotted to them. Though subjects in the curriculum are followed in those periods, these periods are allotted for life-time education.

o That is another way of making them aware of the need of literacy… I mean to become literate

Not only the need of literacy, we teach them in that how to lead a proper life, how to adjust oneself to the society, how to behave with elders. It's a sort of moral education.

o What is the typical first language taught to children?

Bengali.

o At home and also at school?

Both.

o What are all the languages used to teach in the school setting? Not only Bengali?

No, Bengali. Bengali, English and Sanskrit.

o Sanskrit is their third language. What are the medium of instructions—Bengali? In English class, what do they do?

In English class it is English.

o Does the teacher communicate in English?******

The teacher communicates in English but in order to make them realize (they are first-generation learners and they don't even follow the question papers properly), the teacher uses Bengali in English class also.

o   Since you said, you teach your children how to behave in the society, which also an important aspect of literacy, how does everyday literacy look like outside of the school (according to you)?

This is a principal question.

o   As a teacher, what do you feel?

In our country, what is the definition of literacy?—one who can read, write his/her name is a literate. In such a country, how can answer such a question, I don't know. Everyone is literate in this city—Kolkata, everyone. Everyone can write their names. Either in Bengali or in English. That is all they know.

o   But literacy is not only this. There has to be something more. Don't you feel that to become literate they have to know how to read as that is an important aspect of literacy? Don't you feel that?

That is true, but your question was something different. Would you please repeat the question?

o   How does everyday literacy look like outside of the school?

My answer is sufficient, I believe, because what I mentioned is that literacy in our country means only those who can their names. If that is taken into account, then in our city even in my school also, people are literate. But, do they consider literacy as a part of their life, if the question is such, I will say they don't. Literacy programs are being undertaken by the government. But that is not sufficient, I feel. Even if I consider the parents of my children, I mean the children of my school, they are not bothered what they do in school, what they study. They don't even encourage their children to study in the future.

o   Now, after the implementation of the Right to Education Act?

This is a girls' school. So when they reach the seventh or eighth standard, they are encouraged to get married. If there is a proper negotiation (negotiated marriage), they are married off and they discontinue with studies. And we also cannot encourage girls who are below 18 years of

9

age, to continue with studies after their marriage as there is a problem. These are adolescents and when a married girl comes in contact with others, there are certain problems and it is illegal in our country (making a child get married before 18 years in case of girl and 21years in case of a boy).I can't support an illegal act. But I do not go to lodge a complaint with the police. This will lead to a big harassment. I do not allow them to attend classes. But in case of students in classes XI and XII, they are allowed to attend schools if they are married.

o   But this Right to Education Act which has been taken up by the Central government, do you think that it will help more people to become literate?

I am going to be frank with you. My personal view is that this may not happen. This will only encourage more and more people to join the primary sector of our economy that is agriculture. Because they are allowing all the students to be promoted. They are being promoted without taking any rectification measure till Class VIII. Even now this Act has not been taken up by the State government. It will be functional after April 2011. What will happen is that the students after Class VIII i.e. in the ninth standard, will discover that they know nothing. In Class IX, one has to pass in all the subjects. A student who is weak and promoted every year to every class, till Class VIII, one fine morning he will know all the subjects?! It is not possible. So I think after the eighth standard the number of drop-outs will increase enormously. What will they do? They will wait for one or two years and they join either as an agricultural laborer or in the city they will work as laborers. That's it.

o   Why is it important to be literate(in our country)?

In our country there is such an economic background that people are exploited by the rich ad number of poor people, they are much more than the rich sector. So if they are not literate, they probably cannot fight for their rights. So I think 'literacy' has got a great meaning for people in our country.

o   What are some of the strategies used to teach reading in your school? Like Bengali they know. But they are starting English from Class V.

No, from Class I. So when they come to our school, classes V to XII, they already know how to read and write—both English and Bengali. But in the seventh standard they have to take a third language (Sanskrit), which they are taught in class how to read and write.

o   What are some of the challenges the teachers in our country face making the children literate?

The picture is totally different in the urban and rural sector. It is very difficult to bring students to school in the rural sector. They are poor and the number of members in the family is much more. There are more mouths to feed. And the people are generally working in the fields. So manual labor is essential. When a boy or girl of 10 or 12 years old can work, they earn money, they can feed people, and their parents do not feel it necessary to send their children to school. But in the urban sector, people have somehow felt the necessity at least that they should continue their studies up till the eighth standard, so that they can take up a job in an institution, or as a clerk, or in a primary school as Group D staff, they are sending their children to school.

o   But do you feel that the teachers face challenges in case of first-generation learners in making them learn, how to read?

They(teachers) do because they(learners) have never seen their parents even going through the newspaper. Most of the students in our school don't take newspapers at home. So it is not easy to make them understand how to read. But it is also not a challenge of teachers in my school. But you can say that in the primary section of the school they do face some problems. But since the medium of instruction is Bengali, the teachers and the learners can overcome them.

o   But the problem regarding reading…

Reading is different. In the senior school there is no such problem as by then they know the alphabets, they know the words. They know how to pronounce them.

Mrs. Nandita Roy(Teacher of Chetla Girls' High School)

o   What difficulties are you facing in making them learn how to read?

They have their education throughout in their mother-tongue (Bengali). But suppose they are reading a chapter, it has been observed that they fail to understand meanings of many words. So while reading a passage, they are doing it mechanically and hence this reading has no effect on them. And this problem in reading is persisting even in Class XI. This is the case even in their mother-tongue.

o   So how do you encourage them? We teachers have to guide the child to overcome this problem.

Particularly there are problems with certain terms in geography. The question came on the distribution of coal. In Bengali it was written *bɔːntɔːn*(distribution). The girls could not understand as they were not familiar with the word.

○ So how do you try to overcome this problem?

When we take their classes, we try to deal with the terms like *bɔːntɔːn*. So if we try to make them familiar while teaching with these terms, then probably we can get rid of this problem. Even they have problems in expressing themselves also.

○ Even in Bengali (mother-tongue)?

In short questions they are doing well but in descriptive type of questions, they cannot express themselves.

○ So what are the strategies you are adopting in teaching reading?

Actually we have to do it in such a manner that they should understand it properly. They should not write it mechanically. When they are reading something, if I make them understand the matter, then they face no more problems. They are first-generation learners and have no help at home. The same thing happens even during the exam. They know the questions. But if they have problem with the terms, they can understand if we explain. We teachers always encourage them to read a lot of other books other than text books as it will enhance their power in language.

○ But it is a problem for first-generation learners to get books other than text books. How do you solve this problem?

No, we have a library. We provide them with books. And you know that this generation has apathy towards books in general.

Sima Singh (a student of Class XI in Chetla Girls' High School)

○ What is your name?

I am Sima Singh.

12

- Which class are you in?

  I am in Class XI.

- Which stream have you taken? Commerce, Arts(Humanities)?

  I have taken up Arts.

- How many members are their in your family?

  My mother, father, uncle, aunt. I have an elder sister who is married.

- What does your father do?

  My father is a driver.

- Are you the first one in your family to attend school?

  No, my sister also went to school.

- What problems have you faced in your studies till Class XI? You have friends here who have parents to guide them in their studies. But in your case it is never so? So how did you overcome your hurdle in the first Board Exam in Class X? Who helps you if you get stuck anywhere while reading? (Sima feels shy) There is nothing to feel shy about it.

  Whenever I have problem, I go to people living around in my area and who can read and they help me.

- What does your mother do?

  She is housewife.
- Your teachers also help you. Tell me how they do that. You could not have reached this stage without the help of your school.

  Whatever is taught in class I try to follow. I take help(from teachers). At home also I take help(as told earlier).

○ Do you take private tuition?*******

No.

○ What do you do while reading an English book? You should be facing more problem in that language as it is not your mother-tongue.

It is the same process I follow in that language. We have some *dada* (elder brother, but here she meant those elder young ones leaving in her locality), they help me.

Ahead: Ms. Anita Sarkar (School-in-charge)

○ First, I would like to know your name.(Mrs. Sarkar preferred that I spoke to this senior teacher)

I am Shukla Banerjee, Senior Coordinator of Ahead School. I am in this field more than 15 years.

○ I would like to know as a language teacher how you help these special needs children to read and to communicate.

For reading we are mainly following to processes. One who can identify the alphabets and then go into the normal curriculum. The alphabets are taught phonetically. And the others are doing it in Bengali. In English we follow only the functional words which they find in our environment and which they should know to move around. The words are selected according to their mental state and their age like push, pull, in, out, toilet etc. They see these types of words and they will the functions of those words. In Bengali we introduce the alphabets and some of the functional words --- the words which will be interesting for them. I choose those words which will initiate the learning. In case of Anurag (a mentally impaired boy), I choose the names of father, mother (both in Bengali and English) as he will be interested to know the relations. He can show the card and pronounce the word. They do not know the exact alphabet 'b' but they know the word 'baba'(father). In Bengali gradually they learn 'ɔ *to o* '(the vowel sounds in Bengali). This girl here is hearing impaired. She is Swapna. So she has no definite concept of alphabets. She can identify the group word. So there are two processes involved in teaching these children reading—first the alphabet and then the words and the second one is first the whole word and then the alphabets which the child sees in those words. We call it the link word and the individual like 'key' to 'key', 'glass' to 'glass', 'bowl' to 'bowl'. Then comes matching object with picture. Then picture with picture and then picture with name. So in my class they have the picture matching, identification of picture and then picture matching with word.

o   I would like to know, are they able to read books gradually?

Actually that also depend on the mental level. In my class mostly they are moderate level and they are not able to read the books. They are familiar with the functional words. I have introduced you to Anurag. He can identify the words from the books even of they are smaller than those in the cards. He can identify in this way: 'Bābá tʃā khāo', (Father, please have tea),

'Mā dʒɒl dāo' (Mother, please give me water). He can explain the words and they know the verb words also. Anurag, please tell me *Ki lekhā āchhe?*(What is written there?). Anurag says, 'Bābá dʒɒl dāo' (Father, please give me water). Anurag, what is this word? Anurag says, 'tʃā'. Here is Shayan, who is autistic in nature.

o   How long do they stay in school? Till 12.30 p.m.?

It depends on parents. Some parents have difficulties. So they go later than the others.
Anurag is high moderate level but Shayan has no interest to learn many words. He can match nearly twenty words and that is all. Swapna can express through sentence charts but cannot express otherwise.

o   How is reading taught to her?

She is using sign language like for Days like Sunday, Monday she is using gestures, sign language. Here is a communication book for children who cannot express themselves properly. There is another girl who can also see. Her name is Shonai. She cannot express. If I ask her, " Shonai what would you like to do?" She will express through sign language. There is a communication board. There are some noun words and verb words, food item and some expressions written for them. They can easily express their wish through this board. There is coordination between the home and the school in cases of these children who cannot speak. I do not know what she had for lunch. So at home also they are taught the same way. The mother should be involved in this communication book.

○ What support do you think you need from the parents in this case regarding developing their reading habits?

In school they are only for four to six hours. And in one to one session I am getting only one hour or half an hour. Since they are staying mostly with parents, they have o take care of developing the reading habit in them. Shayan has difficulty in understanding as he is autistic in nature. So I told his mother to collect some pictures and show them to him. Like before going to the market, you show your child some pictures and ask him what he like to eat that day. Easily he can show his preference. Or, if she goes to the sweet shop with her son, she can carry that board and ask him which sweet he would prefer. He can identify it and express himself. During tiffin-break, he mainly brings biscuits. So I ask him which he would like—the sandesh (sweet), biscuit. I ask him, you tell me which you would like to have and I will give you. He follows these orders.

○ What are the problems you are facing as a teacher in developing their reading habits?

What we are doing here in the classroom, they are not always following at home. That is causing main problem. This is due to lack of initiative of the parents, proper materials, proper timings. My language class is for one hour. The children get bored if it is too long as they have a short span of concentration. The parents have to take more initiative and care in developing the language skill. We are the special educators. We know the way of teaching and that has to be followed at home by the parents. We are guiding the parents how to do it at home.

Mrs. Dolu Bhowmick (Mother of Anurag Bhowmick)

○ As a mother of Anurag, how do you cope with the situation? How are you helping him to come out of the problems he has in developing reading abilities?

He has no such reading ability as such. English spellings like 'cat', I mostly to do it phonetically. Then it is easier for him to write. He cannot read on his own. When I teach him the spellings, he can follow the words.

○ What else are you doing to develop his habit of reading books though the main orientation is done at school?

We buy newspapers like Ananda Bazar(Bengali daily) and The Telegraph(English daily) everyday. He sees his father, his sister reading newspapers. He immediately sits with The Telegraph ad starts reading the headlines. I do not need to guide him. He can read both the big and small letters.

Mrs. Saha (Mother of Deep Saha- an autistic child)

○ Knowing Deep's problem as his mother, how do you initiate at home his reading habits?

He is not keen at reading. I do not know whether he is afraid of reading. He does not want to school and this is his daily routine. While coming to school also, he keeps on saying, "Mama, I will do a little bit of coloring, a little bit of writing". I make him do matching, coloring but for a short span. Deep can write well, but he refuses to do that. He does not even wish to look at books. He loves roaming around watching everything. Whenever I go to the shop, I take home and make him pay the bill. I give him the money so that he can count and pay. He loves to communicate with people and guests coming to our house. He is more than 9 years old and has not yet been able to complete the alphabets.

Mrs. Ghosh Chowdhury (Mother of Shayan Ghosh Chowdhury)

○ What problems you face in developing his reading abilities?

Academically, Shayan is good. His behavior is the key problem. He cannot tolerate me interacting with anyone other than him. But he is interested in studies and he can understand the time every evening he sits with his studies (around 18.00hr). He brings his books immediately.

○ How do you help him?

I make him sit at 18.00 hr. He has a private tutor at home. He can do addition and subtraction, read write and spellings. He knows the multiplication tables till 6. He can also read simple sentences in English. If I draw a picture of a ball and a bat and ask him to describe where is the bat or the ball. He will immediately answer me in English. He can look at the picture and write the sentence—The ball is beside the bat. He used to go to St. Xavier's' School in Orissa.

17

It is an English-medium school. So he is more interested in English rather than Bengali. The school did not tell us at the beginning. But we could realize that there is a problem. Then we shifted our base to Kolkata (Calcutta) and took him to Monovikas Kendra (an institute for special needs' children). They detected his autism. He tries to avoid reading Bengali.

Wahed Memorial G.S.F.P. School: Mrs. Hasina Banu (Teacher-in-charge)

○ Since this is a high school, from which class do you have here (Madrasah)?

From Class V till Class X.

○ How are the children helped to learn to read? After completing till Class IV, they are coming to your school, isn't it?

We teach them how to read and ask questions to find out if the chapter is understood by them. 50% of my students who are coming to my school are non-literate, though they attend till Class IV. Since it has become a rule that every child should be promoted to the next class, it has become a problem for us. This time we have retained a few extremely weak students in Class V. They have no conception in any subject, they do not know even how to read. Such children cannot cope up with the syllabus of Class VI.

○ Didn't the parents of those children come to meet you?

Yes, they did. We told them the conditions of their wards.

○ Aren't they coming from the junior section of the school which is adjacent to this building? Why is their condition still so poor?

The basic problem lies in the system in education system (RTE Act). The schools are forced to promote certain students, who are not up to the standard of the school. They will get stuck in Class VIII for sure as to get promoted in Class IX, they need to pass in all the subjects. For last three years, we continued with the program according to the rule set by the government. But this year, we were forced to take action.

○ What is the medium of instruction in this school?

Urdu. We have also Bengali as third language and English as second.

o The reading process in English and Bengali is totally different from that of Urdu. In that case, how much effort does the teacher need to give to her learners to teach them reading?

They are beginning with English in Class V. They are already aware of the English alphabets since Class I. They are staring Bengali in this school.

o Please tell me your method of developing the handwriting of the children.

We give them dictation which serves two purposes(conception of spellings and handwriting). The children also get handwriting as homework.

o How many students do you have in the senior section?

Around 350 student (she again said 260 students approximately). New admissions are going on.

o Is the admission process in the junior section handled separately?

Yes.

o Do you have children with special needs in your school?

Yes, we have two physically impaired children in Class VIII. One could not sit for his exam as he had to undergo an operation. The girl is good in studies.

o Are your teachers giving special effort to teach them?

Yes, they are taking care of them along with other children in class.

o What is the duration of each period in your school?

The duration of the first period is 45 minutes and then each is for 40 minutes.

o   When does your school begin?

Our school begins at 7.30 in the morning and ends at 13.00hr. There is half an hour break for lunch.

o   Are your children coming from only Urdu-speaking families?

Yes.

o   What measures are your teachers taking to teach them English Language? The children can understand Bengali as they hear it everywhere outside the family and the school. What about English?

There are teaching materials given by the government but their speaking power is not improving. But it is still hard for many of them to read even after becoming aware of the alphabets in Class I. The English teacher is trying hard but the communication is not that good.

o   Your school has an autonomous body. As the teacher-in-charge are you taking any initiative to overcome this problem?

No, we have no such initiative to develop the skill in English Language, we are only concerned about the syllabi.

o   What are teaching aids used by you in the school?

Books, blackboard and chalk.

o   Do you have computer learning facilities for children?

No, not yet. The management is trying to introduce computer.

Mr. Osman Ali (Head Master of Primary Section)

o   How are the classrooms in your school organized for learning?

There are several teachers. At first I give them instructions, how to teach the children. The school begins with an assembly. After that every children(read child) are segregated according to their classes. They go to their classes. The Class Teacher goes to the class., asks her/his learners a few questions and then begins the routine of the day.

o What are the languages you teach in your school?

Urdu.

o Only Urdu?

This is the mother language (read mother-tongue). This is an Urdu-medium school. But we teach English also.

o And no Bengali?

In Class IV we provide an extra language—Bengali.

o The reading and writing process of Urdu is totally different from that of English and Bengali. How do you teach your students reading English and Bengali?

It is our instruction to all our teachers that when they go to take English class, every teacher is bound to talk in English. Because if the children are not understanding and if you say something from the gesture or expression like you are calling a child—*Come here, go there, stand up*, we try to communicate. After that we prepare the atmosphere for the children to communicate and understand.

o The teacher is trying to create the atmosphere by talking to them in English.

They are capable. They don't think that English is a tough language. We take(read know) the capacity of the children. Suppose when they took birth, they did not know what is the language. In a Christian family, they learn to speak the language by 2 or 3 years. It is our instruction to the teachers to talk in English. We have 45 minutes for English period. In a week they have four to five classes, and in Class IV they are capable to understand, what I say.

o What about reading? How are you teaching your children to read English?

We tell they that A, B, C, are English letters. We tell them that Urdu starts from right-hand, English starts from left-hand. I tell them, you don't afraid. As we have our alphabets, they have their alphabets. In our school we do quiz contest, coming week , and every question will be asked in English and they will answer in English.

o   In the early years, what kind of technology do you use to make them read both Urdu and English?

There is no Nursery class. We start from Class I. Some are below 5 years of age. First we teach them letters. When they know the letters, they start reading.

o   Do you use any special technology?

We use TLM, teaching-learning materials.

o   What are these?
o
(after a pause) It is not possible to say. When you come next week, I can show you.

o   You don't have to show me. You just tell me, what are those?

We have charts with alphabets like A for apple, B for ball, C for cat, D for doll—they are reading. After that there are plastic materials. We ask them to select like where is C. They come to know.

o   Do you have children with special needs?

No, no these type of children we do not keep.

o   What are the learning materials provided to the young learners?

They have books, TLM and Lesson Plan.

o   Lesson Plan is for the teacher, but for the students?

We use teaching materials. At first we teach them rhymes. After they understand, what we are saying, they come to know words. After words they will come to know the sentences. They will learn to say in small sentence.

○ Could you tell me, why it is important to be literate in this world?

Very very necessary. Education is very necessary. Without education it is not possible to live in this society. This is the English world. This is a poverty area and Muslims live here. They are so backward, because they not take care of their education. It is very necessary to send their children to school. Education is necessary for the development of the nation.

○ What are the some of the challenges the teachers are facing while teaching reading?

Challenges, problems we are facing from the poverty area. There are many people. Twenty years English was stopped in the state. It was bad for the children because everybody have to know English. Even the parents who have no conception in English, they try to send their children to English schools. There are many small schools having no future. But they are wasting the children and the guardians are sending their children to those schools. Though we are a government school, they send children to those schools. Now the government is taking steps to teach English and we are also teaching English. In our area Wahed Memorial is one of the best schools. We have quiz contests here. There are schools like South Point and other good schools, but still the Bournvita Quiz Contest Company told us they found our school good. They appreciate our children. We try to satisfy our children and our guardians.

FREED: Mr. Somenath Pyne: Member of the Managing Committee
Mr.Kajal Sharma (Teacher)was interviewed at Mr. Pyne's request

○ If classrooms exist, how are they organized for learning?

Our school in the village is different from that in the city. The school has building made by the government. The government has given benches, books and mid-day meal. But the facility is not enough. Most of the students belong to the daily wage-earners. They are below poverty line. And NGO FREED with its base in the village helps by providing educational support and also take care of the children's studies in the morning before going to school since the children come from backward families. They are most excluded and they are given extra care.

23

○ What does students' handwriting look like?

The children usually come to the school from the age of 5 or 6 years and continues till Class XII. Care is taken for both Bengali and English handwriting. Their handwriting is good.

○ What kind of technology, if any, are the children using in the early years?

Books, copies, chalk, pencil, blackboard and pen are the only things the children are using in our school.

○ What are the learning materials provided to the young adolescent learners?

The learners have text books printed and distributed by West Bengal government.

○ How are difference in language and dialects addressed in school?

Every district in West Bengal has its own dialect which is different from the literary language. While reading the teachers use literary language. If the children do not understand any word, it is explained in local language. But the students use literary language while writing.

South Point School: Mrs. Dalbir Kaur Chadda(Principal)

○ If classrooms exist, how are they organized for learning in your school?

I would say, we have a very organized system. Each class is divided into 14 sections and since we run two sessions, we have seven sections in the morning and seven in the afternoon for each class, except for Nursery class which has five sections in the morning and five in the afternoon. This is how the classrooms are divided.

○ What does the typical school day look like?

A typical school day looks like in any other school, how it functions. It has the children, the teachers, the support staff coming in, in the morning. The teachers and the support staff have to reach earlier before the children in, 10 minutes before. And since we have different timings for different classes, early morning at 6.55, we have the classes I-V coming in, and later on in the day we have Transition, Nursery I and Nursery II. And of course, afternoon session of classes I-V starts at 12.15 p.m. followed by Transition and Nursery classes.

o   What does the print in a book look like?

The printing is clear. To a certain extent bold also so that children can read easily. May be the print becomes little smaller as they go up(to the higher classes).

o   What does student handwriting look like?

Initially, the children just learn to scribble and gradually they are taught to write. Till Class I they write in print form and Class II onwards they start writing the cursive form.

o   What kinds of technology, if any, are students using in their early years?

Well, there are different methodologies. We have play-way teaching, teaching through story-telling, where the children can see and learn. And there are different teaching aids like the Smart Class, where the children view and learn. Besides, teachers also use other educational aids to teach the children.

o   What are the learning materials provided to young learners?

They are provided with text books, information through the computer, through books. Teachers share some information which is not there in the text book and sometimes they also ask the children to go and view on the Internet a few topics. They are asked to do project works to get information.

o   How do you accommodate students with special needs?

Frankly, our school is not very well-equipped, so we try not to take in children of special needs. But sometimes there are a few who have a little hearing difficulty, vision is not that good, so we try to help them as much as we can.

o   How are difference in language and dialects addressed in school?

Dialects are not spoken by the children of Kolkata (Calcutta). Our children are multi-lingual. Initially, when they come in, we try to speak their mother-tongue, so that they can understand and get settled down and then gradually, we teach English. They also have to learn Vernacular---either Bengali or Hindi.

o   What are the major beliefs regarding language and literacy? If more than one, which drives practices in the classroom?

Well, mostly English is like first language in our school. So we insist more on English. But it is not that the other two languages—Bengali and Hindi are not given importance. They too are. But more emphasis is given on English.

o   Yes, but what are the major beliefs regarding language and literacy? How do you connect language and literacy?

If you don't know the language, like you have to surf through the net, everything is available in English. So we feel it is more important for the children to learn the language. It will be easier fir them when they grow up, because that's the world around and they can access any information all over the world.

o   What is the typical first language taught to children at school?

Initially as I said, they are first taught through their mother-tongue. But gradually it is weaned off. Like, you are saying *boʃe dʒāo* in Bengali and simultaneously you are saying 'Sit down', so simultaneously both the languages are taught. They are gradually weaned off from t he mother-tongue.

o   How is literacy defined/perceived in your country?

In our country majority of the people do not get this facility at times, of course there is a change. There was a time when very few people had the advantage. Now, more and more people have the advantage (to go to school). They are more aware and they are trying to learn. You will find people who are helping at home, want their children t o study. I think that is a big thing which our country has progressed.

o   Why is it important to be literate?

If you are not literate, you will be nowhere because to move around in the society, you have to be literate. That's the scenario today. More and more people are becoming literate today. If you have to keep up with the society, if you have to be knowledgeable, you have to be literate.

o   What are some of the strategies used to teach reading?

We encourage reading right from Nursery level. Initially the children hear stories from the teachers and that is a form of reading. And through the story-telling method, we arouse the interest in the children to read. Later on, they are made to read in the classrooms, there is a library period, they are given books. When they go to classes IV and V, they even go to the school library, where they get books issued. And that is how their interest is aroused.

o   What are some of the challenges facing teachers in your country?

One big challenge is because of the Internet coming in, because of the television, because of mobiles children have started moving away from books. They do not want to read. Earlier for any information, we had to read books, now everything is available through the net. As a result the children have stopped reading. Stories which they have read earlier will now see on the television in the form of serials or movies. So they have moved away which is not a good thing. So we in school try to motivate in reading. That's a big challenge.

o   Well, you can say that as your school caters to a different sector of the society. What about literacy in general?

I think in general also, problem is all over India. It is not a problem only of our school because same issues are everywhere. It is not just located in our school.

Mrs. Gopa Barman(ex-teacher and ex-additional Vice Principal)
o   How is literacy defined in your country?

I have very little to say for I have no official data with me. But what I see around, I get a very dismal picture. Even the poorest of the poor in our country, to whom even having one square meal a day is more of a concern, cannot think of literacy. A huge number of people in my city like most of the part-time maids, most of the taxi drivers, vendors are illiterate. How literacy can be spread among them is a serious problem. I am sure the government is trying to do something about it, but how and when they are going to get, I have no idea.

- Why is it important to be literate?

Literacy is the ability to read and write. Achieving this power means the opening up of an entire new world. You now no longer depend on some one else to read out a letter to you or to write a reply to its sender. The key to this freedom is literacy. Literacy changes your vision and alters the way you look at the world. The hoarding for instance, which so far had been a colorful picture with meaningless scribbles, suddenly turns into an area with a significant message for you. They often see that knowledge can be more easily derived through T.V. I think this issue needs to be scrutinized. At least some of the facts, ideas and opinions appearing on the television, may have come from a certain individual groups or institutions, whereas a versatile reader can from his own knowledge and his own opinion through reading. He has now a mind of his own. He now knows himself, his surroundings and also how to communicate his ideas through writings. So to me literacy is a learning that needs a true perspective, enables us to do away with lots of age-old inaccurate assumptions. It helps to judge the world around us and empowers us to choose and reject accordingly. In a nutshell, literacy is empowerment to me.

- What does everyday literacy look like outside the school?
Whatever literacy has derived in my country at least in my state, is only derived from home or from school. This is my perception. The schools can be government or private. Apart from these the Municipal schools which used to cater to slum children previously, have seized to exist now. This results in the sorry state of literacy in our urban area.

Conclusion:

India has tried and is still trying to address the issue of literacy by amending its Constitution in order to make quality elementary education the fundamental right of each and every child. The last two decades have shown a positive growth as the average rate in literacy figures has increased praiseworthily. There is evidence as number of private-run schools mushrooming in the urban areas. But this does not imply that each child especially in the remote villages have equal opportunities in acquiring education as their counterparts living in the city or even towns.

My paper has tried briefly to trace the literacy drive in my country. There are vast disparities in imparting education between government, private schools and the religious schools and the methodologies used by these types of schools. Each and every educator and management members of different schools have come to this conclusion that education acts as a persuasive tool in the emancipation and empowerment of human race and thus leading to the advancement of the nation. It enables us not only to gain knowledge about the world, but also helps us to get positive self-esteem, self-confidence and helps us to face the world. It also helps the human society to eradicate misunderstandings between different races, cultures and religions and thus lead to a world brotherhood. They have also agreed that parental education is necessary for the advancement of a country.

From the interviews it is evident that only the private-run schools provide their learners with modern technologies besides books, pens/pencils and blackboard. The government schools required to be brought up at par with their counterparts. Till now few can access the best education in this country in lieu of money. Those who can, become global citizens with the benefits of English education and a good education system. While a child in a private school can make full use of the modern amenities, the child going to a government school, even in urban areas, has no access to them, let alone the rural areas. The teachers are also trained in the former type of schools to teach their learners with the aid of computer. This computer-associated teaching-learning process arouses interest in children to know more on any topic in any subject. The districts do not even have proper trained teachers to teach the backward children. It is evident from the video clipping of FREED, that an English teacher can teach his learners how to read even the second official language of India (English). But are those poor children learning the pronunciations, which form the base of any language? Some researchers and educationists have strongly advocated the use of mother-tongue as children face problem. Acharya Ramamurti Committee made a recommendation on this parity, "…the fundamental problem in our system is caused, not by a minority of schools but by the majority of schools, namely by the two categories that are fully supported by public funds, the Government schools and the Local Body schools. These have, by and large, remained outside the purview of any real educational audit, though they are required to submit many forms of how small amounts of money are spent. Abolition of the private schools, urged by several persons, will not solve the major educational problem, we feel. It can only be solved when the majority school sector finds it possible to substantively raise its present level of educational attainments and effectiveness."

Sulagna Mukhopadhyay
Teacher-Researcher
Calcutta, India

References

Articles:

(1) Internet: www.indiacurrentaffairs.org: Sen, Amartya: *60 years of Indian Republic: Past and Future.*

(2) Internet: en.wikipedia.org/wiki/National_Literacy_Mission_Programme: *National Literacy Mission Programme—Wikipedia, the free Encyclopedia.*

(3) Internet: lawmin.nic.in/ncrwc/finalreport/v2b 1-5.htm: Ramamoorthy, K: *Literacy In The Context Of Constitution Of India.*

(4) Internet: www.census.gov/ipc/prod/wid-9801.pdf: Velkoff, Victoria A.: *Women's Education In India.*

(5) Internet: www.educationforallinindia.com/page139.html: *Analysis of Census 2001 Data-Education for all in India.*

(6) Internet: www.indg.gov.in/primary-education/.../right-to-education-bill:*Right To Education Act---India Development Gateway*

(7) Internet :www.indianmuslims.info/..../syed_najiullah_the_stauts_of_muslims_in_india.html: Najiullah, Syed: *The Status of Muslims in India*

(8) *Annual Report 2006-07, Ministry of Rural Development, Government of India.*

(9) Internet: www.dise.in/Downloads/Use%20of%20Dise%20Data/Meer%20Lal.pdf: Lal, Dr. Meera: *Education-The Inclusive Growth Strategy for the economically and socially disadvantaged in the Society.*

(10) Dreze, J. (2003), *"Patterns of Literacy and their Social Context,"* in Das V. et. al (ed).
